# ON THE CONTRARY
## AND OTHER POEMS

# Miroslav Holub

## ON THE Contrary

### AND OTHER POEMS

translated by
**EWALD OSERS**

foreword by
**A. ALVAREZ**

## BLOODAXE BOOKS

ISBN: 0 906427 75 4 hardback
       0 906427 76 2 paperback

First published 1984 by
Bloodaxe Books Ltd,
P.O. Box 1SN,
Newcastle upon Tyne NE99 1SN.


Bloodaxe Books Ltd acknowledges
the financial assistance of Northern Arts.

Typeset by
Tyneside Free Press Workshop Ltd, Newcastle upon Tyne.

Printed in Great Britain by
Unwin Brothers Ltd, Old Woking, Surrey.

# Acknowledgements

These poems are taken from two Czech collections, *Naopak* (Prague, 1982) and *Interferon čili o divadle* (forthcoming). Those from *Naopak* appear on pages 15 to 63, and those from *Interferon čili o divadle* on pages 64 to 124.

Acknowledgements are due to the editors of the following publications in which some of the translations first appeared: *International Portland Review, London Magazine, New Statesman, Poetry Review, Prospice,* and the *Times Literary Supplement.* Some were broadcast by BBC Radio 3 on *Poetry Cambridge* (1983) and *In the Test-tube: Miroslav Holub* (1984).

# Contents

15    Brief reflection on cats growing in trees
16    Brief reflection on accuracy
17    Brief reflection on the theory of relativity
18    Brief reflection on the word Pain
19    Brief reflection on an old woman with a barrow
20    Brief reflection on Johnny
21    Brief reflection on Charlemagne
22    Brief reflection on gargoyles
24    Brief reflection on killing the Christmas carp
25    Brief reflection on laughter
26    Brief reflection on the Flood
27    Brief reflection on test-tubes
28    Brief reflection on light
29    The Minotaur's thoughts on poetry
30    Brief reflection on maps
31    Brief reflection on death
32    Brief reflection on childhood
33    Brief reflection on a fence
34    Brief reflection on eyes
35    Brief reflection on the sun
36    Brief reflection on dwarfs
37    The dangers of the night
38    Attempted assassination
40    Theatre
41    The Minotaur's loneliness
42    Minotaurus Faber
44    The Minotaur on love
46    On Sisyphus
47    On Daedalus
48    The philosophy of autumn
49    The old people's garden
50    Whaling
52    Homer
53    On the origin of football
54    On the origin of 6 p.m.
56    At home
57    Dinner
58    A philosophy of encounters
59    Elsewhere
60    On the origin of the contrary
61    On the origin of memory

62    On the origin of full power
63    Conversation with a poet
64    The soul
65    Burning
66    Sunday
67    United Flight 1011
68    Dreams
69    The last night bus
70    A lecture on arthropods
71    Immanuel Kant
72    Biodrama
73    Distant howling
74    Jewish cemetery at Olšany,
      Kafka's grave, April, a sunny day
75    When the bees fell silent
76    Half a hedgehog
78    Interferon
84    Collision
86    Memo to a pre-school-age daughter
88    Landscapes
89    The man who wants to be himself
90    A well-read man
      *or* A meeting with Russell Edson
92    The dead
93    A lecture on diseases
94    Swans in flight
95    Teeth
96    The cast
98    The beginnings of the puppet theatre
100   Punch's dream
101   Punch, the Princess, Johnny and other children
      watch the cheerful play of the kittens
102   Sir Rudolph, the knight
103   Faustus
104   Marguerite
105   In the box
106   Princesses
107   The sorcerer's lament
108   How we played the Gilgamesh epic
111   The autumnal bus
113   The Angel of Death
116   Crucifix
119   Supper à la Russell Edson
122   Sand game

# Foreword

Since Miroslav Holub's poetry first appeared in English in 1967 he has gained a large and curiously proprietorial audience; on both sides of the Atlantic he is read as if he were one of ours. And perhaps he is, since an art that begins and ends in privacy and silence—the poet bending over the blank page, the reader poring over the written words—has become such a minority concern that poetry and its audience now form a single embattled republic, not restricted by national boundaries and languages. Poets like Miroslav Holub, Zbigniew Herbert, Vasko Popa and Sándor Weöres have become in translation part of our common literary world—not foreign, just different—all of them engaged, like the rest of us, in a game without frontiers.

For Holub, the transition into English has been particularly smooth, and not only because he has been extremely lucky with his translators. He also brings to poetry the habits of mind of a scientist. He takes clarity and common sense for granted and uses language as he would use a slide in an experiment: as a transparent medium in which to fix the specimen—the event, the moment, the feeling. Although he has his share of beautiful images—'Swans in flight' begins 'It's like violence done to the atmosphere; as if Michelangelo reached out from the stone'— his colloquial voice and rational manner would be clear and direct in any language. They also leave him nowhere to hide; in the limpid air of his poetry there is no place for evasion or illusion or fakery. Either confusion is fixed and distanced by the scientist's precision—'when I kiss you/ your tongue tastes/ of a tenth planet, a parthenogenetic one'—or reason doggedly reasserts itself, willy-nilly—'Then came the tea-break./ And I realised/ that hysteria doesn't solve anything.'

At no point in his career has Holub seemed to treat poetry as a soft option, an escape from the detail and discipline of his scientific work. Instead, he dignifies both his vocations by bringing to bear on them the same method—observation—and the same attitude of mind—doubt. The only difference is that the poet is wider-ranging and freer than the scientist, drawing imaginative conclusions from the most sober data, sometimes with such determination and ingenuity that he seems to be using one discipline to challenge the other. 'Brief reflection on an old woman with a barrow', for example, begins like a scientific text book, complete with equations, and ends with a kind of agnostic prayer—that is, the equations are followed through until they appear to explain the whole world. Observation and doubt. Scientific doubt that questions each conclusion until it can be proved experimentally becomes, in the poetry, ironic dissatisfaction that undercuts clichés, generalisations and every grandiose claim made in the teeth of experience. All that is left is the individual, observed and observing, the reasonable man, vulnerable and full of doubt. Holub the poet makes notes on life in much the same spirit as Holub the clinical pathologist writes notes on an experiment: coolly, quizzically, yet alert to every implication, open equally to the world of fact and the world of feeling. And like the scientist, the poet draws conclusions; he becomes a moralist, rationally, whether he wants to or not, because that is where the evidence leads him. For instance, 'The dead' begins with a brief description of two old men suffering from the same disease; one died full of optimism and appetite, the other hung wanly on 'through eight insipid years'. The poem ends: 'I know they died the same way./ But I don't believe they are/ dead the same way.' The pathologist knows death because he knows the intricate mechanisms of the living cells; the poet judges between the styles of death because he is an expert in the subtleties of living.

Holub, who was born in 1923, did not begin to write poetry until he was thirty, at the same time as he began his research in immunology. For the last thirty years his two careers have flourished together equally. As a scientist, he has a solid international reputation; as a poet, his intelligence, wit and vulnerability, his clarity and unflagging distaste for whatever is pretentious or second-hand has made him one of the most original and certainly one of the sanest voices of our time.

A. ALVAREZ

# ON THE CONTRARY
## AND OTHER POEMS

# Brief reflection on cats growing in trees

When moles still had their annual general meetings
    and when they still had better eyesight it befell
    that they expressed a wish to discover what
    was above.
So they elected a commission to ascertain what was above.
The commission despatched a sharp-sighted fleet-footed
    mole. He, having left his native mother earth,
    caught sight of a tree with a bird on it.

Thus a theory was put forward that up above
    birds grew on trees. However,
    some moles thought this was
    too simple. So they despatched another
    mole to ascertain if birds did grow on trees.

By then it was evening and on the tree
    some cats were mewing. Mewing cats,
    the second mole announced, grew on the tree.
Thus an alternative theory emerged about cats.

The two conflicting theories bothered an elderly
    neurotic member of the commission. And he
    climbed up to see for himself.
By then it was night and all was pitch-black.

Both schools are mistaken, the venerable mole declared.
    Birds and cats are optical illusions produced
    by the refraction of light. In fact, things above

Were the same as below, only the clay was less dense and
    the upper roots of the trees were whispering something,
    but only a little.

And that was that.

Ever since the moles have remained below ground:
    they do not set up commissions
    or presuppose the existence of cats.

Or if so only a little.

# Brief reflection on accuracy

Fish
    always accurately know where to move and when,
    and likewise
    birds have an accurate built-in time sense
    and orientation.

Humanity, however,
    lacking such instincts resorts to scientific
    research. Its nature is illustrated by the following
    occurrence.

A certain soldier
    had to fire a cannon at six o'clock sharp every evening.
    Being a soldier he did so. When his accuracy was
    investigated he explained:

I go by
    the absolutely accurate chronometer in the window
    of the clockmaker down in the city. Every day at seventeen
    forty-five I set my watch by it and
    climb the hill where my cannon stands ready.
    At seventeen fifty-nine precisely I step up to the cannon
    and at eighteen hours sharp I fire.

And it was clear
    that this method of firing was absolutely accurate.
    All that was left was to check that chronometer. So
    the clockmaker down in the city was questioned about
    his instrument's accuracy.

Oh, said the clockmaker,
    this is one of the most accurate instruments ever. Just imagine,
    for many years now a cannon has been fired at six o'clock sharp.
    And every day I look at this chronometer
    and always it shows exactly six.

So much for accuracy.
    And fish move in the water, and from the skies
    comes a rushing of wings while

Chronometers tick and cannon boom.

# Brief reflection on the theory of relativity

Albert Einstein, in conversation—
  (Knowledge is discovering
  what to say)—in conversation one day
  with Paul Valéry,
  was asked:

Mr Einstein, how do you work
  with your ideas? Do you note them down
  the moment they strike you? Or only
  at night? Or the morning?

Albert Einstein replied:
  Monsieur Valéry, in our business
  ideas are so rare that
  if a man hits upon one
  he certainly won't forget it.

Not in a year.

## Brief reflection on the word Pain

Wittgenstein says: the words "It hurts" have replaced
    tears and cries of pain. The word "Pain"
    does not describe the expression of pain but replaces it.
    Thus it creates a new behaviour pattern
    in the case of pain.

The word enters between us and the pain
    like a pretence of silence.
    It is a silencing. It is a needle
    unpicking the stitch
    between blood and clay.

The word is the first small step
    to freedom
    from oneself.

In case others
    are present.

# Brief reflection on an old woman with a barrow

Given an old woman and given a barrow.
I.e. the system old woman O and barrow B.

The system is moving from the paved yard Y to the corner C,
 from the corner C to the stone S, from the stone S
 to the forest F, from the forest F to the horizon H.

The horizon H is the point where vision ends
 and memory begins.

Nevertheless the system is moving
 at a constant velocity v,
 along a constant path,
 through a constant world and
 a constant destiny,
renewing its impulse and its meaning
 from within itself.

A relatively independent system:
in landscapes from horizon to horizon
always just one old woman with a barrow.

And thus we have, once and for all,
 that geodetic unit, the
 unit of travel there and back, the
 unit of autumn, the
 unit Our daily bread, the
 unit of wind and lowering sky, the
 unit of the distance home, the
 unit As we forgive them, the
 unit of nightfall, the
 unit of footsteps and dust, the
 unit of life-fulfilment Amen.

# Brief reflection on Johnny

The above-named, as is well-known, coming
    from a poor but honest background,
    set out across nine mountains and nine
    rivers to see the world.

There
    he became the victim of myths. In reality,
    as of course we all know, he did
    in the Black Forest meet the white old man and exchange
    a few words with him;

However,
    he gave him nothing since by then his cake had been
    polished off by the dwarfs.
    He went on, sadly, into the city but
    he couldn't hear any story in any tavern
    since

All taverns had been closed by royal decree
    and strangers, after questioning under duress,
    were speedily escorted to the Dragon's Rock.

There he met the dragon which, without further ado,
    gave him a thrashing and made him sign a contract
    that he would lure all passing knights-at-arms
    into the dragon's claws.

The princess and half the kingdom were things he had to
    invent when he was captured on his flight
    by musketeers and when he had to explain
    his lengthy absence.

And so he came back home impoverished and emaciated,
    in rags and totally without illusions. He sat down
    amidst the hay in contemplation. It was then
    that he discovered that all of a sudden
    he understood the speech of birds and flies,

And listened to them with complete comprehension.

And from the red-backed shrikes he learned
    some really pretty fairy-tales.

# Brief reflection on Charlemagne
*(see Julius Zeyer's tale of the same)*


Outside the gate
hangs a bell. Charlemagne, son of Pepin the Short,
had it placed there. Those who have suffered injustice
strike it and Charles interrupts his king-business,
receives them at once, hears them out, and dispenses justice.
That was in AD 800.

This year the bell rang.
In the rain, which was
a cloudburst rather than a drizzle
and had been continuing for eleven hundred years,
soaked to the skin, drenched, like a drowned rat,
in a fool's motley
stood Charlemagne.

In broken Frankish he urgently pleaded
for a hearing.

# Brief reflection on gargoyles

In the course of general petrification cliffs grow
    from diatoms, cities from sighs and
    imperatives from question-marks.

In the course of general petrification angels resident
    in pointed-arch portals, among finials and
    slender turrets rigidify into solid
    sulphurous devils, with desperate claws catch hold of
    cornices and thus become gargoyles.

In this role
    they start to open their mouths at those passing
    below, saying:

What are you gaping at, clot,
    or else
Dust thou art, to dust returnest,
    or sometimes
Better watch your gravitation.

When it rains they pour out their spite in copious streams,
    shaking with pleasure and contempt,
at night they lick the earth with spongy tongues,
    turning white into black
    and vice versa.

But sometimes in spring they feel ashamed of themselves,
    climb down, and in the shape of black cats and
    moon-struck dormice
    with yowls they criticise the Gothic style and
    gargoyles in particular. Then inquisitive angels
    without portfolios descend from on high
    and, clinging to the cornices with desperate claws,
    they listen. And so they, too, go rigid
    and sulphurous, and petrify.

The above procedure thus ensures
a perpetual exchange of gargoyles,
the unchangeability of Gothic façades
and a respect among all passers-by, cats and dormice

for gravitation.

# Brief reflection on killing the Christmas carp

You take a kitchen-mallet
and a knife
and hit
the right spot, so it doesn't jerk, for
jerking means only complications and reduces profit.

And the watchers already narrow their eyes, already admire the
          dexterity,
already reach for their purses. And paper is ready
for wrapping it up. And smoke rises from chimneys.
And Christmas peers from windows, creeps along the ground
and splashes in barrels.

Such is the law of happiness.

I am just wondering if the carp is the right creature.

A far better creature surely would be one
which— stretched out— held flat— pinned down—
would turn its blue eye
on the mallet, the knife, the purse, the paper,
the watchers and the chimneys
and Christmas,

And quickly

say something. For instance

These are my happiest days; these are my golden days.
Or
The starry sky above me and the moral law within me,
Or
And yet it moves.

Or at least
Hallelujah!

# Brief reflection on laughter

In laughter we stretch the mouth from ear to ear,
    or at least in that direction,
    we bare our teeth and in that way reveal
    long-past stages in evolution
    when laughter still was an expression of
    triumph over a slain neighbour.

We expel our breath right up from the throat,
    according to need we gently vibrate our
    vocal chords, if necessary we also touch our foreheads
    or the back of our heads, or we rub our hands or slap
    our thighs, and in that way reveal long-past stages
    when victory also presupposed
    fleetness of foot.

Generally speaking, we laugh when we feel like laughing.

In special instances we laugh
    when we don't feel like laughing at all,
    we laugh because laughter is prescribed or
    we laugh because it isn't prescribed.

And so, in effect, we laugh all the time, if only
to conceal the fact that all the time someone
is laughing at us.

# Brief reflection on the Flood

We have been brought up with the notion that
    a flood means
    water rising beyond all bounds,
    engulfing fields and woodlands, hills and mountains,
    places of temporary and abiding stay,
so that
    men and women, meritorious oldsters
    and babes in arms, as well as the creatures of field and forest,
    creepies and heebee-jeebies,
    huddle together on rocky pinnacles
    which slowly sink into the steel-grey waves.

And only some Ark... and only
    some Ararat... Who knows.
    Reports on the causes of floods differ most
    strangely. History itself is a science
    that's based on poor memory.

That kind of flood needn't worry us too much.

A real flood
    looks more like a puddle.
    Like a little swamp nearby.
    Like a leaky washtub.
    Like silence.
    Like nothing.

A real flood means that balloon-bubbles
    come from our mouths
    and we think they are
    words.

# Brief reflection on test-tubes

Take
    a piece of fire, a piece of water,
    a piece of a rabbit or a piece of a tree,
    or any piece of a human being,
    mix it, shake it, stopper it up,
    keep it warm, in the dark, in the light, refrigerated,
    let it stand still for a while—yourselves far from still—
    but that's the real joke.

After a while
    you look—and it's growing,
    a little ocean, a little volcano,
    a little tree, a little heart, a little brain,
    so little you don't hear it lamenting
    as it wants to get out,
    but that's the real joke, not hearing it.

Then go
    and record it, all dashes or
    all crosses, some with exclamation-marks,
    all noughts and all figures, some with exclamation-marks,
    and that's the real joke, in effect a test-tube
    is a device for changing noughts
    into exclamation-marks.

That's the real joke
    which makes you forget for a while
    that really you yourself are

In the test-tube.

# Brief reflection on light

We make light so we can see.

In the Silurian they made light to see the Silurian.
In the Diluvium they made light to see the Diluvium.
In Troy they made light to see Troy.
And that's how they spotted all those Greeks around them.
In the Enlightenment they made light to see the Enlightenment.

The same applies today.

Indeed
certain species developed, such as fireflies,
or occupations, such as torch-bearers.
A lot of energy is converted into light,
electrical and chemical, mechanical and biological.
Even a battery is sometimes found.
So much light has developed that we can see round corners,
that we can see into our stomachs,
that we can see into the little roots of night.

Not that seeing is any particular
fun.
But we've got to see in order to
make light,
            light,
                    light,
until we go blind.

# The Minotaur's thoughts on poetry

Certainly this thing exists. For
on dark nights when, unseen,
I walk through the snail-like windings of the street
the sound of my own roar reaches me
from a great distance.

Yes. This thing exists. For surely
even cicadas were once of gigantic stature
and today you can find mammoths' nests
under a pebble. The earth, of course,
is lighter than it once was.

Besides, evolution is nothing but
a long string of false steps;
and it may happen that a severed head
will sing.

And it's not due, as many believe, to
the invention of words. Blood
in the corners of the mouth is substantially
more ancient and the cores of the rocky planets
are heated by the grinding of teeth.

Certainly this thing exists.
Because
a thousand bulls want to be
human.
And vice versa.

# Brief reflection on maps

Albert Szent-Gyorgi, who knew a thing or two about maps,
   by which life moves somewhere or other,
   used to tell this story from the war,
   through which history moves somewhere or other:

From a small Hungarian unit in the Alps a young lieutenant
   sent out a scouting party into the icy wastes.
   At once
   it began to snow, it snowed for two days and the party
   did not return. The lieutenant was in distress: he had sent
   his men to their deaths.

On the third day, however, the scouting party was back.
   Where had they been? How had they managed to find their way?
   Yes, the men explained, we certainly thought we were
   lost and awaited our end. When suddenly one of our lot
   found a map in his pocket. We felt reassured.
   We made a bivouac, waited for the snow to stop, and then
      with the map
   found the right direction.
   And here we are.

The lieutenant asked to see that remarkable map in order to
   study it. It wasn't a map of the Alps
   but the Pyrenees.


Goodbye.

# Brief reflection on death

Many people act
as if they hadn't been born yet. Meanwhile, however,
William Burroughs, asked by a student
if he believed in life after death,
replied:
—And how do you know you haven't died yet?

# Brief reflection on childhood

In the turquoise-coloured fields of childhood there's nothing
  except childhood.

Nor is there anything in the yellowing sky, nor
  on the bare ochre wall, nor behind the bare ochre wall,
  nor on the oriental horizon, nor beyond the horizon,
  nor in the little house, nor on the target, nor in the mirror,
  nor behind the mirror.

Except childhood.

Objects are strange and unfamiliar because they were there
  before and will be there after. So far as I remember,
  childhood is solitude amidst
  a confederacy of things and creatures which
  have no name or purpose.

Names and purpose are thought up by us afterwards. Then we believe
  that the wall divides something from something else,
  that the house provides shelter from stormy weather and
  that the nightingale spreads happiness by song and fairy-tales.

That's what we believe. But it probably isn't so.

For the emptiness of houses is boundless, boundless
  the fierceness of nightingales, and the path from gate
  to gate has no end anywhere.

And seeking we lose, discovering we conceal.
For we are still searching for our childhood.

# Brief reflection on a fence

A fence
    begins nowhere
    ends nowhere
and
    separates the place where it is
    from the place where it isn't.

Unfortunately, however,
    every fence is relatively
    permeable, some for small
    others for large things, so that
the fence actually
    does not separate but indicates
    that something should be separated.
    And that trespassers will be prosecuted.

In this sense
    the fence can
    perfectly well be replaced
    with an angry word, or sometimes even
    a kind word, but that as a rule
    does not occur to anyone.

In this sense therefore
    a truly perfect fence
    is one
    that separates nothing from nothing,
    a place where there is nothing,
    from a place where there's also nothing.

That is the absolute fence, similar to the poet's word.

# Brief reflection on eyes

Goddesses, gods, fear and Twiggy have very large eyes.
Some gods, in fact, have such large eyes that nothing was left for
   anything else and that god *is* the eye.
The Eye itself then sees everything, knows everything, and grants
      gifts
which admittedly would be granted even without the Eye, but with
   the Eye they're a lot better.

Cyclopses, olms, informers and the angels of the Apocalypse have
very small eyes. But a lot of them.
One small eye at every keyhole.
Certain angels and their equals in rank, by which we don't mean
      the olms,
have such small eyes that not even a fragment of man
fits into them.
These eyes then drop their lids for concealment.

Behind the eyes are the optic tracts and the occipital lobes of the
      brain,
where individual areas correspond to individual areas of the retina.

Behind excessively large eyes lies nothing.
Behind excessively small eyes sits the Apocalypse.

# Brief reflection on the sun

Thanks to the systematic work of our meteorologists,
and altogether thanks to the general labour effort,
we have all been witnesses of many solstices,
    solar eclipses and even
    sunrises.

But we have never seen the sun.

It's like this: we have seen the sun
    through the trees, the sun above the Tatra
    National Park, the sun beyond a rough road,
    the sun drenching Hašek's village of Lipnice,
but not the sun,
Just-the-Sun.

Just-the-Sun, of course, is unbearable.
Only the sun related to trees, shadows,
    hills, Lipnice and the Highway Department
is a sun for people.

The Just-the-Sun hangs like a fist over the ocean,
    over the desert or over the airliner,
    it doesn't cast shadows, it doesn't flicker from movement,
    and is so unique it almost isn't at all.

And it's just the same with truth.

# Brief reflection on dwarfs

In the far world
a great many dwarfs
have become by far the greatest
dwarfs in the world.

Already a Superlohengrin approaches
on a superswan, to the choir of a
supercigar which has acquired
the permanent wedding march.
Geological strata of petrified
dreams and words thunder underfoot.

In the near world
a barely perceptible
Snow White drags herself along mouse tracks,
searching for seven honest old
dwarfs,

such as would
still feel ashamed
under the magnifying glass.

# The dangers of the night

Bedroom; a double bed; ceiling; bedside table; radio.
And outside darkness propped up by the trees
beneath which a dark blue jaguar is prowling.

The walls part and the double helix
of oneness
pervades the shadowy breathing of the roof.

Perhaps a galaxy. But more probably
the whites of eyes giving a hint of wind.

The enemy is approaching: the black image,
the image of oneself
in the mirror, sleep. His hands
are growing and his fingertips are
touching.

Resist. For in the morning,
in the naive light of songbirds' brains,
he that wakes will be
someone else.

## Attempted assassination

He walks through the town like
an indigestible remnant
on the tongue. Ticking away in his pocket
is the infernal machine, to be
flung or placed
at the right moment, at the right spot.

His shadow appears to him
like a fuse-cord stretching
through history, from war to war.
His body appears to him
like the fulcrum of a balance
on which our age
tips the scales

and centuries shall be put
to flight.

He clutches his infernal machine
to his heart, closer and closer,
so it dissolves his skin,
so it dissolves its metal,
the one permeating the other.

Now the infernal machine is inside,
and ticking and ticking, and when
it at last seems that this is the street,
and this is the house, and this is the moment
in the funeral cortège of our days
he reaches inside, but
it can no longer be pulled out,
yet it is ticking, and hurting,
and he takes to his heels,
fleeing from the ticking,
fleeing from himself,
losing his shadow and losing the town,

finding himself on the plateau
of an unsetting sun,
an unmoving sky, and
immersing himself in the settling
precipitate of clay,
leaving an outline

of body or explosion,
a temporary body and a permanent explosion.

On Sunday a family
takes a walk in those parts.
Can you hear it? asks the little boy,
poking a stick in the clay.

No one hears anything.

Drop it this instant,
says the father to the boy
who in his hand triumphantly
carries

a dead mouse.

# Theatre

Only sorcerers believe that the theatre is a mingling of the blood of the poet with the blood of the actor. The simple magic of the theatre is in the fact that an empty space which signifies nothing is entered by people with tickets and by people who tear off the tickets, and by people in overcoats and people without overcoats, and by people who know it all by heart and by people who don't know it by heart yet.

They have all read the inscription THEATRE and for a while they act accordingly.

For that period of time everything signifies something. Even the space, even the hush, even the breath, even the blood, even the shadow.

One of the troubles with the world is that the inscription THEATRE is found in so few places.

# The Minotaur's loneliness

Walls. Walls. A voice. A word
uttered weeks before returns
years later,
with its other self.

Walls. Walls. Fear. Shadow
of a shadow fearing a shadow.
As we... Do not forgive.

Walls. Walls. Fragments of fragments,
amphorae from which for seven years trickled
images of seas dried up but for their roar.

Walls. Walls. And perhaps
not even walls. Perhaps I'm merely walking
on an imaginary ground-plan,
unable to do otherwise:

To turn aside would mean there was no Minos,
there was no Crete, there was no Theseus.
Only an ageing Ariadne
on the cliff's edge awaiting
her fall.

# Minotaurus Faber

Whenever I come to the table
I neatly lay out my tools
(small hammers, pliers, anvils and small shafts),
I draw a diagram, in red and black,
upon the infinite white surface of beginning,
I start to join and bend, rivet and solder,
hammer and scrape, the blows ring out
from depth of soul to depth of soul,
concentric rings are widening and I
am at the centre, at the very centre.

Already a small machine is taking shape,
a fledgling machine, transmissions, firing-pins,
windings and spools, attraction and repulsion,
here and there it ticks, here and there
it listens,
we're nearly there,

when from down under me rings out the sound of hooves
pounding upon the savage granite
like drums in black festivities,
hammering of arteries, tightening of muscle and the pull
of tendon straps (hands only turned to wood),

the body rearing towards the sky's grey murkiness,
charging through corridors and passageways
in frantic ecstasy.
(Small grains of metal scattered by the mane):
We're far now, far past the abyss.

I roar and race, I demand
the fairest of princesses,
in order to... dishonour and devour her
with bloodiest tenderness, and all I see
is those hooves, hooves,
hooves towering over
a naked body.

Only thus can I forget,
though I don't rightly know
what.

# The Minotaur on love

The love of the Centaurs is eternal
like being broken on the wheel.

That night, however, when Ariadne
gave Theseus that fateful thread
(and I could see them, for the labryrinth's walls
recede and open at the equinox)
(and I could see them, for I was Theseus
just as Theseus
can be me)
that night they faced each other
and his hands rested
upon her shoulders:

their features were dark
as the waves of the Styx and
their bodies were of stone.
They stood and up above them stood the moon
and stood the sea.
And it was clear that love is not
in movements but
in a kind of menacing
endurance that escapes from time.

At length they turned transparent and
the worms could be seen gnawing
deep within them: she knew then
that she would die on Naxos
and queue for olives as if that
were the meaning of life,
he knew that he would die in Athens,
a king of the theatre
with ten mistresses
and cirrhosis of the liver.

But then they stood, his hands upon her shoulders,
and up above them stood the moon
and there stood the sea. And I,
faced with that love,

I dug my bull's head
into the sand and in some unfamiliar
despair I smashed the walls
and roared O Theseus, Theseus,
I'm waiting for you, Theseus,
and then the labyrinth flung back at me the words
and my own
Homeric laughter.

# On Sisyphus

Unable to roll up that boulder,
that boulder or whatever it was, maybe gneiss, maybe paper,
I decided the fault lay with me.
The important thing about faults is they can be corrected,
my mother used to say.

I decided the fault lay with me.
So I added to the boulder
as much weight again. Whatever it was,
maybe hate, maybe love.
And at once it went better. Because

of the certainty that it would
probably break my neck.

Then came the tea-break.
And I realised
that hysteria doesn't solve anything.

# On Daedalus

Daedalus potters in the labyrinth.
Self-generating walls.
There's no escape.
Except wings.

And all round—those Icaruses. Swarms of them.
In the towns, in the plains, on the uplands.
In the airport lounge (automatic
goodbyes);
at the space control centre (transistorised
metempsychosis);
on the sports ground (enrolment of pupils
born 1970);
in the museum (blond seepage
of beards);
on the ceiling (a rainbow stain
of imagination);
in the swamps (hooting of night,
born 1640);
in the stone (Pleistocene finger
pointing upward).

Time full of Icaruses,
air full of Icaruses,
spirit full of Icaruses.

Ten billion Icaruses
minus one.

And that even before
Daedalus invented
those wings.

# The philosophy of autumn

The late sun's rays
with gentle fingers touch the yellow leaves
outside. Reflected in the window are
a book and a silhouette and a
silhouette, a halo of fair hair;
we are this year
permeated with history
as a cobweb with light.

I ask myself if the prevailing
shortage of geniuses
may not be caused by the disappearance
of tertiary stages of syphilis.

Some kind of heavenly spider
rises above you, above me
and above the aspirin.

# The old people's garden

Malignant growth of ivy.
And unkempt grass,
because it no longer matters.
Beneath the trees an invasion
of fruitful Gothic.
Dusk had fallen, mythological
and toothless.

But the Minotaur beat it
through a hole in the fence.
The Icaruses were caught
somewhere in spiders' webs.

In the dawn's early light
the disrespectfully grey, insolent
frontal bone of fact
is revealed.
And it yawns without word.

# Whaling

There is a serious shortage of whales.
And yet, in some towns,
whaling flotillas drive along the streets,
so big that the water is too small for them,
or at least a harpoon sneaks
from pavement to pavement,
searching.
It finds.
The house is stuck. A creature elementally
thrashes about and the blood diffuses
in the sky's white eye.

And that is the Old Testament incident,
the primal drama,
the basic event,
to be harpooned and dragged away,
between seaweed and cod,
    between primers and copy-books,
between algae and trawl nets,
    between mugs and mother's photographs,
between slippers and cobwebs in the corner,
between the ship's keel and the sea's keel,
    between the morning and the evening hour,
harpooned and dragged away for the greater glory
of the gods of harpooning and dragging away,
harpooned and dragged away to eternity
to the stifling inwards roar of blood
which tries to resist and with frantic claws
hangs on to the drops from the water tap,
to the reflections on the window pane,
to the first childish hairs
and fins.

Yet there's nothing left but waves and waves
and quartering
on that anonymous other shore,
where there is neither good nor evil,
only the scraping of elastic bone,
the peeling-off of plaster, revealing

older and older medieval frescoes,
the stripping of the skin, revealing
the sliminess of a foetus just conceived.

And now the whistle's painful unison sounds,
the whalers' music,
the fugue which towers in one spot
like an obelisk of a last breath
behind the curtain.

No one has written
that whales' Antigone, the whales' Electra,
the Hamlet of the whales or their Godot,
the whales' Snow White, or even
*One Flew over the Whales' Nest,*

although the whale is itself
a kind of metaphor.

Metaphors face extinction
in a situation which itself is a metaphor.
And the whales are facing extinction
in a situation which itself is a whale.

# Homer

Seven cities contend to have harboured his cradle:
*Smyrna, Chios, Kollophon,*
*Ithaké, Pylos, Argos,*
*Athénai.*

Like a lamb he strolls
through marine pastures,
unseen, unburied,
unexcavated, casting no
biographical shadow.

Did he never have trouble with the authorities?
Did he never get drunk? Was he never bugged,
not even when singing?
Did he never love fox terriers, cats,
or young boys?

How much better the Iliad would be
if Agamemnon could be proved to bear
his features or if Helen's biology
reflected contemporary facts.

How much better the Odyssey would be
if he had two heads,
one leg,
or shared one woman
with his publisher.

Somehow he neglected all that
in his blindness.
And thus he towers
in literary history
as a cautionary example
of an author so unsuccessful
that maybe he didn't exist at all.

# On the origin of football

A small pebble embedded in concrete:
a statue to the genius of earthworms,
not budging at all.

A small milestone of history,
such a tiny little
triumphal arch
where nothing has ever happened:
not budging at all.

A small rheumatic post
from which someone has stolen the notice
forbidding the stealing of notices:
not budging at all.

An electrified wire
barbedly garrisoning
the dreams of shin ulcers:
not budging at all.

And so, when one day someone encounters
something that's rolling
he kicks it.

And his heavens reverberate,
the temple curtain is rent,
the unrinsed mouths of thousands open wide
in a stifling explosion of silence

like trilobites
yelling *Goal*.

# On the origin of 6 p.m.

> Human names are
> simplified by names.

The day, gnawed by the sun,
tossed among the dummy houses:
we walk, dragging our love behind us
like a big croaked dog.
> But how many lives have been saved
> by mouth-to-mouth resuscitation?

And that is all, that vacuum-sealed vanity?
That talk of herrings in an undated tin?
Certainly. And we hold our fork
in the left hand and put the bones
on the side of the plate, for eternity.
> Your eyes, of course, are neon
> and wherever you look a fiery
> writing appears on the wall.

There are no words. There never were
when it came to the crunch. On the threshold of fate
poetry is silent, choked
by its own bitterness.
> Fortunately I hardly ever
> understand you.

We write upon each other with scalpels,
like a Chinese poet drawing with a brush.
Some blood coagulates quickly,
some flows and flows.
> The magnitude of things
> is measured by the depth of the cut.

We cross on the red light. Because the game
is without rules; and many years ago
they plundered our chessboard squares,
so nothing but the snoring of the kings remains,
and shouts of pawns and neighing of knight's horses:
and on all these we are enjoined to silence.

But when I kiss you
your tongue tastes
of a tenth planet, a parthenogenetic one.

And that is all, that claw of darkness?
These suicides of sleep, from which
we awake right under the stone?
And that is all, that examination
of skeletal remains?
      Your gait indeed is royal:
      frightening infallibility of breasts.
      You walk without motion.

We live by hope. Certainly. Its
parasites gnaw in the brain's emulsion.
A latent image is left.
Sometimes not even that.

And so it's six o'clock
this day. The same as yesterday.
The same as tomorrow.

## At home

At home we register the existence of a pernicious rampant growth, of lethal mutations or self-destructive diseases in the body of the world without uneasiness or vertigo. Home is a place of immunity provided that everyone has changed into slippers in the hall and that the gravy contains the customary amount of cornflour.

Home is a state in which the photograph album is a source of immortality and the image in the mirror persists without limit, like a butterfly in a beam of light.

Home is a semi-lethal mutation of the world with the emphasis on the prefix semi-.

## Dinner

That soup's to be eaten up to the last spoonful because that's where all the goodness is.

Eat up that lovely soup, don't mess about with it!

Else you'll be weak and won't grow up.

And that'll be your fault.

Just as it is the fault of towns and nations that they've stayed small.

I blame the small nations for not having become powerful. So much the worse for them.

*Ich beschuldige die kleinen Nationen...*

*Accuso le piccole nazioni...*

*J'accuse les petites nations...*

Come on, get that soup down before it's like ice!

# A philosophy of encounters

A train which is the mirror image of another train. A handshake from window to window. A cordial talk between very close people in windows moving parallel away from each other.

—Next time—

—Yes, next time—

—Next time we meet—

—Yes, next time we'll meet next time.

Whereby next time means last time and last time is last time only because it could be next time.

Every process in nature can, under the same law, unroll also in reverse: the principle of parity.

Of course the principle of parity does not apply to weak interactions.

# Elsewhere

A journey, like changing from one rib-cage
into another, air pressure pressing from above
and below, we contract,
we're in the capillaries, barely capable of
the main stream, hidden, vainly
sought by the news and vainly seeking,

embryos trembling with the breath
of non-existing Fates.

After a while the mollusc in us
pushes out its shapeless head: it is waiting for
the postman
with a white letter
with the definition of fog,
known also as the natural state of affairs.

The postman comes. He has green eyes,
a bag containing kisses on the forehead,
some fingerprints
and registered mail.

The postman passes by and calls nextdoor.
Gently and calmly
a tornado rises.

We are flooded out
we are exposed

and we left
our brolly
at home.

# On the origin of the contrary

Like the sky breaking up –
but it was only a pair of hands.

For a while it beat its wings
but the hands closed
even more. The wings resisted.
It scraped its feet but the hands
closed and one leg broke off.

Each time it moved something
the hands closed and something broke off.
So it kept rigid. It might have been
catalepsy.

But it might have been a creeping realisation
that there's no longer any blue.
                            On the contrary.
That there's no longer a meadow with flowers
here and there.
                  On the contrary.
That there's neither glucose
            nor rustling
            nor time
                        but on the contrary.

And that's how things stand. Until
someone gets tired of it. This life,
this death, or that tickle on the palm.

# On the origin of memory

The day dawns over the sea.
The polyps are singing.
But what remains are
old and new
assuredly lacerating
coral reefs.

Song is and is not.

But what remains
after all that bleeding?

A hermetic theory
of the blood clot.

# On the origin of full power

This time,
when houses sit on eggs
of a small Easter death
and a symphony orchestra lies
in ambush under the bushes,

when drums and trombones
pounce on people in the park,
demanding alms in excess of
live body weight,

he listens to a no longer familiar
internal unison,
to his storm in a teacup,
to his And yet and yet,

from the quick little flame
he does not recognise the big city,
he realises the weariness of the mountain mass
face to face with a falling stone

and this time at least
when asked replies:

Yes, I can.

And he goes his way
of the flute.

## Conversation with a poet

Are you a poet?
    Yes, I am.
How do you know?
    I've written poems.
If you've written poems it means you *were* a poet. But now?
    I'll write a poem again one day.
In that case maybe you'll be a poet again one day. But how will
you know it is a poem?
    It will be a poem just like the last one.
Then of course it won't be a poem. A poem is only once and
can never be the same a second time.
    I believe it will be just as good.
How can you be sure? Even the quality of a poem is for once
only and depends not on you but on circumstances.
    I believe that circumstances will be the same too.
If you believe that then you won't be a poet and never were a
poet. What then makes you think you are a poet?
    Well—I don't rightly know. And who are you?

# The soul

In Queen's Street
on Friday night
—lights only just blossoming
but already with the pomegranates
of shows for adults only—
among the herds of cars
a yellow
inflatable balloon
was bouncing about
with what remained of its helium soul,
still two lives left,

amidst the song of armour
bouncing with yellow
balloon fright
in front of wheels
and behind wheels,

incapable of salvation and
incapable of destruction,
one life left,
half a life left,
just a molecular trace of helium,

and with its last ounce of strength
searching with its string
for a small child's hands
on Sunday morning.

# Burning

The fire was creeping along the logs,
whispering curses and incantations.
Then it settled in a corner
and began to grow and to sing.
It found its language
in an old letter
from mother.

Orestes' fire. Antigone's fire.
The terrible fire: it is hot
and the smoke rises to heaven.

## Sunday

The Marathon runners have reached the turning point:
Sunday, that day of sad songs
by the railway bridge
and the clouds.
                    Your eyes, at zenith —
and to say this without using the body is
like running without touching the ground.

            Thirty years ago
a transport passed here, open wagons
loaded with silhouettes,
with heads and shoulders cut out
from the black paper of horror.
And these people loved somebody,
but the train returns empty
every Sunday, only
a few hairgrips
and cinders
on the wagon floor.

Who know how to touch the ground,
who knows how not to touch the ground?

No choice but to believe
in the existence of the Marathon's finishing line
in two hours and forty minutes,
amidst the deafening din of the clouds
and of empty open wagons
on the railway bridge.

# United Flight 1011

Megalopolis far behind,
engulfed by air. Remaining only
a few towers, the din of millions,
the shells on Coney Island beach
and the gentle yielding of your body
in the atmospheric disturbance
called morning.

Thirty thousand feet up
you answered: Yes,
I love you, yes.
Then the sign came up to
Fasten Seat Belts and the B-737
set down for a smooth landing.

Basically, of course, it remained fixed
in the vast white box of the sky
like a butterfly on the pin of a word.

For where would we be
if love were not stronger than poetry
and poetry stronger than love?

# Dreams

They sap man's substance
as moon the dew.
A rope grows erect
from the crown of the head.
A black swan hatches
from a pebble.
And a flock of angels in the sky
is taking an evening class
on the skid pan.

I dream, so I dream.
I dream
that three times three is nine,
that the right-hand
rule applies;
and when the circus leaves
the trampled ground will
once more overgrow with grass.

Yes, grass.
Unequivocal grass.
Just grass.

# The last night bus

The last bus echoes away
in the depth
of night's
spinal canal.

The stars tremble
unless they explode.

There are no other civilisations.
Only a gentle
galactic fear
on a methane base.

# A lecture on arthropods

The mite Adactylidium
hatches in his mother's body,
eats up his mother's body from inside
while mating
with all his seven
little sisters.

So that when he's born
it's just as if he had died:
he's been through it all

and is freelancing now
in the target's bull's-eye,
at the focus of non-obligatory existence:

an absolute poet,
non-segmented,
non-antenniferous,
eight-legged.

# Immanuel Kant

The philosophy of white blood cells:
this is self,
this is non-self.
The starry sky of non-self
perfectly mirrored
deep inside.
Immanuel Kant
perfectly mirrored
deep inside.

And he knows nothing about it,
is only afraid of draughts.
And he knows nothing about it,
though just this is the critique
of pure reason.

Deep inside.

# Biodrama

The puppet king
stages a mounted hunt
for sausages.
Terrified boiling wursts
and bewildered frankfurters
scuttle through thickets,
their fat little bellies
pierced by arrows.

They are close to extinction.
The last specimens
are kept
in refrigerated cages
at the Babylon zoo.

The balance of nature
has again been upset. The knell
has been sounded for the invertebrates.

A few foolish children
are crying.

# Distant howling

In Alsace,
on 6th July 1885,
a rabid dog knocked down
the nine-year-old Joseph Meister
and bit him fourteen times.

Meister was the first patient
saved by Pasteur
with his vaccine, in thirteen
progressive doses
of the attenuated virus.

Pasteur died of ictus
ten years later.
The janitor Meister
fifty-five years later
committed suicide
when the Germans occupied
his Pasteur Institute
with all those poor dogs.

Only the virus
remained above it all.

## Jewish cemetery at Olšany,
## Kafka's grave, April, a sunny day

Searching under the sycamores
are some words poured out from language.
Loneliness skin-tight
and therefore stony.

The old man by the gate,
looking like Gregor Samsa
but unmetamorphosed,
squints in this
naked light
and answers every question:

I'm sorry, I don't know.
I'm a stranger here.

# When the bees fell silent

An old man
suddenly died
alone in his garden under an elderberry bush.
He lay there till dark,
when the bees
fell silent.

A lovely way to die, wasn't it,
doctor, says
the woman in black
who comes to the garden
as before,
every Saturday,

in her bag always
lunch for two.

# Half a hedgehog

The rear half had been run over,
leaving the head and thorax
and the front legs of the hedgehog shape.

A scream from a cramped-open
jaw. The scream of the mute is
more horrible than the silence after a flood,
when even black swans float
belly upwards.

And even if some hedgehog doctor were
to be found in a hollow trunk or under the leaves
in a beechwood there'd be no hope
for that mere half on Road E12.

In the name of logic,
in the name of the theory of pain,
in the name of the hedgehog god the father, the son
and the holy ghost amen,
in the name of games and unripe raspberries,
in the name of tumbling streams of love
ever different and ever bloody,
in the name of the roots which overgrow
the heads of aborted foetuses,
in the name of satanic beauty,
in the name of skin bearing human likeness,
in the name of all halves
and double helices, of purines
and pyrimidines

we tried to run over
the hedgehog's head with the front wheel.

And it was like guiding a lunar module
from a planetary distance,
from a control centre seized
by cataleptic sleep.

And the mission failed. I got out
and found a heavy piece of brick.
Half the hedgehog continued screaming. And now
the scream turned into speech,

prepared by
the vaults of our tombs:
Then death will come and it will have your eyes.

# Interferon

Always just one demon in the attic.
Always just one death in the village. And the dogs
howling in that direction. And from the other end
the new-born child arrives, the only one
to fill the empty space in that wide air.

Likewise also cells infected by a virus
send out a signal all around them and defences
are mobilised so that no other virus
has any hope just then of taking root
or changing fate. This phenomenon
is known as interference.

And when a poet dies in the depth of night
a single black bird wakens in the thicket
and sings for all it is worth
while from the sky a black rain trickles down
like sperm or something,
the song is spattered and the choking bird
sings sitting on an empty rib-cage
in which an imaginary heart
awakes to its forever interfering
futility. And in the morning the sky is clear,
the bird is weary and the soil is fertilised.
The poet is no more.

In Klatovy Street, in Pilsen,
by the railway bridge, there was
a shop with quilted bedcovers.
In times when there's a greater need
for a steel cover over our continent
business in quilted bedcovers
is slack. The shopkeeper was hard up.
Practical men when hard up usually
turn to art.
In his shopwindow, open to the interior
of his shop, its owner built
a gingerbread house of quilts
and every evening staged

a performance about a quilted
gingerbread house and a red-quilted
Little Red Riding Hood, while his wife
in this quilted masquerade was alternately
the wolf or the witch, and he himself
a padded-out Hansel,
or Gretel, Red Riding Hood or grandmother.
The sight of the two old people
crawling about in swollen billows
of textiles round the chubby cottage
was not unambiguous. It was a little like
the life of sea cucumbers in the mud
under a reef. Outside thundered
the approaching surf of war and they
conducted their quilted
pantomime outside time and action.

For a while children would stand outside but
soon they would go home. Nothing was sold.
But it was the only pantomime
at that time. The black bird sang
and rain poured into a rib-cage
wearing the Star of David.

But in the actors under those quilted covers
*l'anima allegra* must have just then awoken
and so, sweating and rapt, they acted
their undersea *commedia dell'arte*,
thinking there was a backstage until
a scene was finished, jerkily they moved
from shopwindow to gingerbread house and back,
with the exuberance of Columbines
stricken by polio, while the music
of fifes and drums did not reach them.

Or else they thought that such a deep
humiliation of the customary dignity of age
interfered with the steps of gentlemen
in leather coats and with
the departure of trains to human slaughterhouses.
It did.

The black bird sang and the ruined
sclerotic hearts leapt in their breasts,
and then one morning when they didn't play
and had not even raised the blind –
the sky was clear, the soil was fertilised –
the quilted bedcovers were confiscated
for the eastern front and the actors
transferred to the backstage
of the world, called Bergen-Belsen.
No trace is left of the shop today:
it's now a greengrocer's with woody parsnips.

Always just one death in the village.
Always just one demon.
Great is the power of the theatre, even if
it always does get knocked down in the end
and flung backstage.

The dogs howl in that direction.
And the butterfly pursues the man
who stole the flowers.

When we did autopsies at the psychiatric
hospital in Bohnice, filled with the
urban exudations of relative futility,
the car would tip us out amidst the ward blocks
whose inmates waved from windows
with some kind of May Day pennants, and then
one went, hugely alone,
beyond a spinney to the solitary morgue, where
the naked bodies of ancient schizophrenics
awaited us, along with two live inmates; one of them
would pull the corpses up from underground
with a rope hoist and place them
upon the tables as a mother might an infant
for baptism, while the other was lurking, pen ready poised,
in a dark corner to write up
the Latin protocol, and he wrote faultlessly.
Neither of them uttered the slightest sound, only
the hoist shaft moaned... and the knife
drawn over skin and dermis made a sound
of satin tearing... and they were always

enormous and unprecedented pneumonias
and tumours big as dragons' eggs,
it rained into the opened thorax –
and in that roaring silence one had to
break the line of an angel's fall
and dictate the logical verdict
on a long-sentenced demon...
and the schizophrenic's pen in the corner
busily scraped across the paper
like an eager mouse.

We need no prompters
said the puppets haughtily.

The air of that anatomical theatre
was filled with interferon,
it was a great personal demonstration
against malignant growth, it was
a general amnesty for the walls, entropy
was abjured for the moment

because there are no bubbles at the bottom
to burst under the breeze.

The red balloon outside rose up
to an unsuspected sky, its chains
strained by the certainty that the nearer the inferno
the greater the paradise,
the nearer the prison cell
the greater the freedom.
*Cantabit vacuus coram latrone viator.*

And that is the weird essence of the theatre
that an actor stripped of everything mounts to
the very top of the conflagration
and everything else dies down, falls silent
like a long-hunted animal, its muscles
still twitching but with endorphines
and an infinite peace in the brain.

Yes, even a whale will sometimes leave the school,
hurl itself into shallow water and perish in the sun

like a levelled cathedral, with pushed-out penis,
and death is instantly buried
in a grain of sand
and the sea laughs.

Go ask the tree-stumps; in broken language
they preach about saplings. And in the jargon
of galactic white dwarfs the stars
of the main sequence shine forever.

In the non-Euclidean curved space,
which eludes understanding as much as
the interference of the theatre,
you ceaselessly hear the voices of children
from the primary school of death,
children from the puppet tragedies of the kitchen
and children from the junketings of war,
when skewering them on lances
with their wriggling little legs
provided spice like curry for the mercenaries,
voices of children eluding understanding –

But we've washed behind our ears,
we've stopped pulling the cat's tail,
we've stopped shoving our fingers
into electric sockets –

What else is there left in the universe
of hominisation, slow as the decay of tritium,
than the doctrine of the growing sense of shame of demons:
since Aztec times high priests no longer
offer up sacrifice while dressed in the skin
of a freshly flayed prisoner.

We need no prompters, they said –

Once on St Nicholas' Day, the man acting the Devil,
dead drunk, fell down some stairs and lay there,
and a child, experiencing that embarrassing
joy mere inches from terror,
ran out after the thump and called:

Mummy, come here, there's a dead devil –

And so he was, even though the actor
picked himself up after another tot. Maybe the dogs howled,
but only by a black mistake.
In the sky shone the stars of the main sequence,
the bird was getting ready in the thicket,
the child shivered a little
from the chill of three million years,
in that wide air, but
they prompted him, poetically,

you're only imagining all this,
look, the butterfly's already
bringing the flowers back... and
there's no other devil left... and
the nearer paradise...

He believed, and yet he didn't.

# Collision

To think I might have been dead,
he said to himself, ashamed, as if this were
a curse of the heart, raising a bundle of bones
to a man's height. As if it were suddenly
forbidden to touch even words that had dropped to the ground.
Besides, he was afraid of finding
his body in a metal press. Embarrassing
down to the capillaries.

The tram stood jammed above him
like an icebreaker's prow and all that was left of the car
was a grotesque pretzel with a chunk bitten off
by the dentures of a demented angel.
Something dark was dripping on the rails,
and a strikingly pale wind was leafing
through a book still warm.

People were forming a circle and with deaf-mute
sympathy awaited the play's catharsis,
like maggots emerging from
under the wings of a beheaded chicken.
From afar came the approaching wail of sirens,
congealing in the jinxed air-conditioning of that day
and that minute. Dewdrops were falling
on the back of the neck like remnants of
atmospheric dignity. Embarrassing down to the capillaries.

No, thank you, he said, I'll wait;
for a silent film had started to run
without subtitles, without colour and without answers.

And what about the magnetic monopoles
escaping seconds after the Big Bang,
protons violating the irreversibility of the flow of time?

What about the giant molecular clouds
under the galaxy's shoulders, conceiving
the embryos of stars?

What about the loneliness of the first genes
accumulating amino acids in shallow primeval pools
at the expense of entropic usurers?

What about the desiccated starfish
like proto-eagles' talons dug into the bed
of a vanishing sea?

What about the mortal migrations of birds
observing the sun's inclination
and the roar of sex hormones?

What about the caged half-crazed
orang-utan who vomits because
he has nothing else to do?

What about the mice which for a thousand years
have learned to sing and the frogs balancing
on one leg like the thigh
of a beauty queen from Mesopotamia?

What about poetry, an enterprise
so disorderly it twists the rulers
and increases the squint of school inspectors?

And what about the little girl
in the leukemia ward who, on the toilet,
tried to show what kind of moustache the kind doctor has,
but as her skinny sticks of hands let go of
the edge of the bowl she falls in and so
tried again and again?

And what about the weak-kneed intellectual,
the professor who understood the approximate universe
but forgot the traffic rules?

No, thank you, he said to some uniform,
I don't need anything. My papers are in my pocket
but I can't reach there. And he tried
to smile a little at this embarrassment of completed creation.
It's all my fault, he said,
thank you.
                    And then he died.

# Memo to a pre-school-age daughter

When no one's watching
behind us
the sky and the rain are rolled up
like music paper with a trumpet part,
houses and squares are tidied away in a box
padded with newspapers,
the birds change into letters
in a secret black book,
puddles reflecting night and distant
fires are stowed away in the attic
like grandfather's presents to grandmother.

The trams are put away in cotton-wool clouds.
Pedestrians go to the cloakrooms
and unwrap their sandwiches:
their walking is over
when no one's watching.
And through the city, on seven long legs
a giant spider stalks and in a whisper
advertises the next scene.

It's interval time in the dubious theatre
of a thousand actors and one spectator.

When you're elsewhere the home left behind
shrinks to a blown-glass crib
under a superannuated Christmas tree.
Dogs with eyes like teacups
and dogs with eyes like millstones
carry off your princess
from the gloomy castle, where
philosophers stand on their heads
and the king puts away his crown,
too heavy for a fool.

Flocks of other children rise
into the branches of the ancient elm
and twitter as they fall asleep.

When you're elsewhere the home behind
is soaked up into a small mirror
and our parents act in a theatre of flies
of which you're unaware because it is
a play within a play
and night's about to fall.

That's why I always cried a little
when we had detention
and home was not in sight.

But now I have got used to it.

Even though
I still don't know the play.

# Landscapes

Yes, you were there. We were supposed to lift beets but the totally drunk engineer kept throwing them straight at us so that we had to dodge them. And he kept inviting you to have a schnapps with him. Morass mixed with hate. The photographer fell into the stream and was badly bruised. An ambulance was on its way.

But in the distance all was peaceful.
Far to the north, up on the plateau
fine smoke. Somebody roasting somebody.

Far to the west
a gathering of hunters, fat
as opossums. Their jaws

were masticating every kind of mammal
and bird, as if to choke the balance of the sky.

Far to the south grey clouds
were copulating and a bolt of lightning
was stuck in the clay,
shaped like a tree.

Then came the farm officials and began to curse because the beet was all over the place. As everybody else was drunk they berated us.

On the field-path by the mouse-hole
bloomed a butterbur confused by
this spectacle of autumn,
although it was all
perfectly obvious.

# The man who wants to be himself

He flings out the plastic flowers and chases away the electric current. He sweeps out all voices and shadows and with two turns of a major key locks them out. Two days and two nights he showers in the dew. He takes an eraser and rubs out all traces of non-self on his self. His skin is now as pink as an embryonic membrane and his soul is lighter than helium.

He floats up over his garden, a toadstool cap on his head and fossil foliage on his shoulders. He collects the teeth of extinct species and places them under his tongue.

Now he is himself, he whispers to himself in the unknown language of the Aztecs.

He extends his hand to shake it, but the hand itself refuses.

He searches for himself under the stones but he just cannot find himself. Not on the bottom, not on the surface, not in the washbasin, not in the mirror and not under the carpet.

I'm probably not worthy of myself, the man mutters.

Perhaps I'd better not admit I'm me.

# A well-read man
## *or* A meeting with Russell Edson

A certain man enters a bookshop because he has decided to stand up to the voraciousness of books. He picks up a book from a stand, looks around, and shakes out the letters. Then he picks up another book and another, and shakes out the letters. Surreptitiously he kicks the little black heap of letters under a bookcase.

He continues, row after row, leaving on the shelves the empty hides of the bound books and the deflated bellies of paperbacks. His eyes shine and his spirit touches the paper stars on the ceiling. He no longer picks and chooses.

But then he comes up against a book with sticky letters. People today are terribly cunning. The letters stick to his hands, they get up his sleeves, they tickle him under his ribs, they crawl over his face. In front he is covered with writing like a page from a newspaper. An initial clings to his flies, the print-run figure sticks to his shoe. He tiptoes behind the stand and brushes himself down. It's no use—the more he brushes himself down, the more letters crawl over him, the more he pats himself the more letters appear because—as might have been expected—suitably matched sticky letters mate when they are agitated and instantly produce young.

How is the lettered man going to get out of the shop?

The lettered man walks up to the pay desk and declares that this is his book, that he himself has written it all over himself. All the remaining books burst out laughing and the man leaves after a payment for overheads and author's tax. But there's no way of getting home. Lettered citizens are not allowed on any public transport, for who the hell can tell what the text means or what's hidden behind it?

So the lettered man makes his way home on foot, through side streets, and the children spell him out.

When he reaches home he is very tired: literature is no lightweight affair. He wants to lie down. But his wife chases him out of the bedroom because letters are crawling out of him like fleas from a dead dog. The wife gets out the hoover and the man beats himself on the carpet rack. You aren't coming indoors like that, says the wife. The man wants to go into the dog kennel but his wife won't let him do that either because the dog might catch the mange from the letters. The man takes some candles, goes down to the cellar and reads himself. And don't you dare come upstairs, his wife calls down to him, till you've read yourself absolutely clean.

The man reads and reads, and his wife is getting the dinner ready from a few steamed poems.

# The dead

After his third operation, his heart
riddled like an old fairground target,
he woke up on his bed
and said: Now I'll be fine,
fit as a fiddle. And have you ever seen
horses coupling?

He died that night.

And another dragged on through eight insipid years
like a river weed in an acid stream,
as if pushing up his pallid
skewered face over the cemetery wall.

Until that face eventually vanished.

Both here and there the angel of death
quite simply stamped his hobnailed boot
on their medulla oblongata.

I know they died the same way.
But I don't believe that they are
dead the same way.

# A lecture on diseases

Diseases of puppets are tiny, thread-like, with soft funereal fur-coats and big ears. And small claw-like feet.

There is no fever. Only the sawdust trickling from their sleeves.

Diarrhoea only like woe from wit.

Cardiac arhythmia only like the tick of the death-watch beetle.

It doesn't even look like disease. More like attentive listening, falling over one's eyes like a hood.

When the strings break, that's the end. All that's left is a wooden peg on the banks of Lethe. And at the crossing the little green man comes on: Walk!

Chin up, calls the puppeteer. We'll do Macbeth, calls the puppeteer. Everyone kicks the bucket in that play anyway. And the remaining puppets obediently line up backstage and tip the water out of their little boots.

# Swans in flight

It's like violence done to the atmosphere; as if Michelangelo reached out from the stone. And all the swans on the entire continent always take off together, for they are linked by a single signalling circuit. They are circling, and that means that Fortinbras's army is approaching. That Hamlet will be saved and that an extra act will be played. In all translations, in all theatres, behind all curtains and without mercy.

The actors are already growing wings against fate.

Hold out—that's all.

# Teeth

Teeth are rather ridiculous remains of the outside inside. Their life is filled with dread that they might find themselves on the outside again and get lost there. A lost tooth doesn't know which way to turn, it doesn't know whether it is clenched or revealed in a smile, it doesn't know how to strike root and thus lose its capacity for aching.

A lot of teeth have been lost during the evolution of civilisations. Either through educational or corrective interventions in the lives of young individuals, or through decay in old age. Teeth knocked out during the evolution of civilisations and cultures do not rot but trudge through subterreanean darkness, afraid to come out into the light. Teeth wearied by their pilgrimage are discovered, thus causing a number of new scientific disciplines to emerge.

The remaining teeth get together on cloud-darkened evenings, trembling with fright and exchanging stories of gums, fists, jackboots and other stomatological implements. These stories are not devoid of a certain unintentional comic element. The teeth become comic figures and repeat their stories night after night, century after century.

That's how the puppet theatre began.

It is a theatre of teeth for which no mouths were left.

So close your mouths, dear children, and pay attention.

# The cast

Punch   (pink costume with jingle bells, especially on his cap; about two feet tall, more or less sexless and lacking adrenal glands; expert on good and evil)

Johnny   (country bumpkin, transparent as a fresh spring, member of the local gymnastic club; helps old ladies across the state highway and collects wild berries and waste paper)

The Princess   (brocade and a tiara of genuine cheap costume jewellery, speaks foreign languages as well as the speech of the common people; she is post-pubertal but still waiting for her dragon)

The Dragon   (genus Agamidae, with many spare parts, well-preserved)

The Water-Sprite Michael   (green, frog-like, freshwater but has often found himself at sea, hence his bronchial and respiratory catarrh)

Little Red Riding Hood   (red cap on fair hair, parents in steady jobs, grandmother an alcoholic)

The Witch   (used to be Little Red Riding Hood herself, she has warts and a burlap bundle; readily multiplies into groups of two to four; fries only with honest-to-goodness fat)

Old Man Škrhola   (rugged but simple-minded, which enables him to have a clear-cut opinion on everything; dressed in a subfusc coat and a sheepskin hat because a man should keep his head out of the wind)

Old Dame Škrhola   (knows her name and address, wears plain national costume; regarded as an expert on the biographies of all the other puppets)

The Sorcerer Gruntorád   (pointed hat and a yellow eye; his cave is in such a mess that minor miracles occur spontaneously)

Doctor Faustus   (full beard to hide a neurotic mouth-twitch; his poodle has already caught it from him)

Matýsek the Cop   (white tunic, blue straps supporting his drum and drumsticks; huge shako with a peak, does not acknowledge civvies; mostly invents his decrees)

Marguerite   (poor thing)

The King   (a king)

Knights, devils and others.

# The beginnings of the puppet theatre

Originally, in newborn and toddler times,
Punch, the size of a near-adult lemur,
would scamper through the meadows, herding his building blocks
and singing dirty songs.
The King ruled over climbing ivy and
the Dragon, bastard son of infusoria and runes,
splashed happily about in a drop of water.

The molecular weight of the Princess was
about 200,000.
Then the sun rose and shadows were cast.
Through natural selection among the shadows
the puppeteer evolved. The puppeteer
decided that it was improper for Punch
to sing dirty songs, for kings to rule over ivy,
for love to be made in drops of water or for
the molecular weight of beautiful women to be measured.
He decided that the proper course would be
for everything to have its line and spine. And so
Punch and the King, the Dragon and the Princess
all had a wire pushed through the tops of their heads,
a long way down.

The massive mess of promiscuous primal procreation
was replaced by the orderliness of dim reason.
Thus Punch turned mute, the King turned idiotic,
the Dragon turned to stone, the Princess miscarried,
and the building blocks scampered all over the world.

And all was silent, void and motionless as
in a museum of hunting trophies.
It was nothing to do with the theatre. Not even
an occasion for folklore.
So the puppeteer fitted strings to the fossils'
hands and feet, so they could be comically jerked,
giving rise to new life. The puppets could grin,
mouths open ear to ear,
multiplied by carving the soft wood,
uttering words of wisdom cribbed by classical authors

from other classical authors.

And the ivy grows and grows, from liver to brain,
from cradle to altar, up the curtain and
down again,

to the effective applause of children who
have never heard of silence and have forgotten
the piercing roar of primal creation.

# Punch's dream

I'll slip out in front of the curtain, taking
great care not to tangle my strings
in the flies,
I'll jingle my bells (merrily),
doff my cap
and before the puppeteer knows what's happening
I'll speak in my own voice,
you know,
my own voice,
out of my own head,
for the first and the last time,
because afterwards they'll put me back in the box,
wrapped in tissue paper.
I'll say what I've wanted to say
for a whole eternity of wood,

I'll say it, no matter how ridiculous
my little voice may sound, how embarrassingly squeaky,
I'll say the most important, the most crucial thing,
I'll speak my piece...

Maybe it will be heard.
Maybe someone will take note.
Maybe they won't laugh.
Maybe it'll grow in the children
and irritate the grown-ups.
Maybe it'll change the colour of the set.
Maybe it'll rouse the cardboard
and the spotlights' shadows. Maybe it'll shift
the laws of relativity.

I'll say... Hi there, kids, you're a great bunch,
say hello to your pal Punch!

## Punch, the Princess, Johnny and other children watch the cheerful play of the kittens


A velvet paw but a sparkling eye.
*Eh bien, n'y touchez pas...?*
Boundless the world of play,
a huge crystal ball
containing the two
(kittens),
dark-gleaming,
milk-tender,
rambling roses
born of a flute,
anxiously seeking the warmth of hands,
writing the world's soft side with little claws,

these two
and a dancing mouse,
whose throat they've bitten through,
still twitching skinny feet.
*Tout de même, ils sont comme nous.*

# Sir Rudolph, the knight

He won the femur fencing bout,
He won the belfry toss, spot on.
He won the 5 x 8 metre race.

He won the quail swallowing event
    and the swan riding.
He won the leap across the Rubicon
    with a half-turn.

He won the blood pouring from bucket
    into the storage tank as well as
    the blood count.
He won the sackcloth quick-change.
He won the love-song contest
    and came top in testosterone production.
He won the entombment
    and the resurrection.
He won the victory-count event.

Then a knot dropped out of his cardiac region.
He was glued up again with flour-paste,
    which is the elixir
    of winners.

# Faustus

Recently
Doctor Faustus
was flung out to the attic.
His performance no longer
satisfactory.

He'd come to believe
he really was Doctor Faustus.

His poodle had croaked.

His apprentice Wagner
delivered the closing speech
and from each word
leapt a hyena.

# Marguerite

I beseech Thee, Lady of Sorrows, look down on my misery.
I am but love, I know nothing else. The gates of hell
yawn beyond the curtain.
I beseech Thee, Lady of Sorrows,
at our one hundred and sixty-second performance
make Heinrich, that's Faustus, be careful. Let him not sign with
    his blood,
let him marry me, let us make love, let the lights be switched off,
let our children without strings and wires
sing unknown songs, resounding
among the paper treetops.

I know it's only a play.
But only a play is stronger
than damnation.

# In the box

The Dragon is licking his wounds.
The devils are keeping each other warm.
The Witch has given the Princess a scarf
the poor girl's always cold.
Punch is biting his nails.
Johnny is snoring.
Škrhola is re-counting his salary,
it doesn't add up.

Now and again
one of them furtively
crawls out of the paper,
finds a piece of wire
and blindly searches for somebody's head.

It's no great matter, he'd merely
like to poke someone's eye out,
to have a souvenir
of this season in paradise.

## Princesses

To trumpet flourishes
and the ringing of bells,
behind drawn curtains
the joyful decapitation
of princesses.

Their bodies are taken
hostage
and their dreams are enacted
independently
on the high ceiling
of the shadow theatre.

And in the morning, naked in the nakedness
of the other person,
we ask ourselves whose hands are these

and from which play came
this immortal scene
from the ancient dynasty
of If.

# The sorcerer's lament

First it was too wet.
      So there was no spell-casting.
Then the fountains dried up, yeast
aborted, water-snakes turned
into watch-chains and watercolours became
the sand of heavenly tracks.
      So spell-casting wasn't possible.

Some years I completed
my tax return on white mice.
The King had a row with the Queen,
wallpaper grew ears, fire
rolled up into linoleum
and lightning struck the piano.
      So it was impossible to tell
      if there was any spell-casting or not.

Eventually there was a total shortage
of bats. I made them out of paper
but they resembled little flying pigs.
And they were eaten up by the thready tapeworms
from the typewriters. My magic wand
got pregnant by a retired saint.
My apprentices took to the bottle.
      So that, in actual fact, I never
      began spell-casting.

But my great magic is
that I'm still here. A medium-grade
halo over both my heads.

# How we played the Gilgamesh epic

Working mainly from the Neo-Assyrian version our puppet-master wrote a play that had no equal in the field of puppet theatre. Our company, he believed, had the right actors for the different characters.

Matýsek the Cop would act the powerful King Gilgamesh. He knows who to handle a drum and drumsticks, which he'll drop, as it were, into the Nether World in Act XII. Enkidu, the hairy forest dweller, will be played by the Devil Marbuel, and the Lady of Easy Virtue, who puts other ideas into Enkidu's head, by the Princess. Dame Škrhola will be perfect as the Goddess Ishtar: she'll just have to shed a few clothes. Utnapishtim, who built the ark for the Flood, will be the sorcerer Gruntorád—without his hat, of course. That leaves us Franz the Footman and Sir Rudolph the Knight for the gods Shamash and Enlil. The only problem we had was with the monsters. So it was decided that Humbaba could be played by old Škrhola wearing the head of the Dragon, and the Bull of Heaven by the rest of the Dragon, whose haunch could be easily unscrewed and flung at the Goddess Ishtar. Hansel and Punch could both undergo a succession of quick changes to enact the remaining goddesses, gods, serpents, wolves, scorpions and the people of Uruk.

To make the play suitable for juvenile audiences the puppeteer deleted all questionable passages, such as Enkidu's fornication with the Lady of Easy Virtue, Gilgamesh's wedding with the Goddess Ishtar, and the ban on sexual intercourse in the city of Uruk. This greatly simplified the action. In the time gained there would be hurdy-gurdy music and the Lady of Easy Virtue would lecture Enkidu on the advantages of a school education.

During rehearsals the puppeteer then decided to leave out also all fights and battles, since their educational value was questionable and they tended to break the puppets' strings. Actually, in the fight between Gilgamesh and Enkidu the Devil Marbuel's nose got damaged, so that his place had to be taken by a hurriedly dug-up Doctor Faustus with Beelzebub's hairy hide stuck on him. These scenes were therefore replaced by geographical lectures given by the Water-Sprite Michael in front of the curtain.

Then it was found that the sets
lacked a cedar forest and the roaring of the Giant Humbaba
        made the puppeteer
lose his voice. The swords
with two-talent blades and their thirty-pound
hilts wielded by both sides
got lost during rehearsals.
The elamak-wood table, the cornelian bowls
filled with honey, the lapis lazuli bowls
filled with butter had not been delivered at all.
To open a trap so that
Enkidu's spirit might waft up from the Nether World,
like a gust of wind, was a technical
impossibility. But the acting was totally dedicated:

Punch and Hansel scamper across the farmyard, yelling:
        Thou hast created Gilgamesh,
        create thou now his likeness.
        Let him stand up to his turbulent heart.
        Let them pit their strength 'gainst each other,
        so that Uruk regain its peace.

In a forest clearing sits hairy Faustus with the Princess,
declaiming:
        I fain would challenge him and boldly speak to him,
        I want to shout in Uruk: I am strong!
        I am the one who changeth destiny!
        I am he that was born in the wilderness, that is blessed with
                strength!
And the Princess says with feeling:
        Eat bread, Enkidu,
        And drink beer, as is the custom here!

Matýsek the Cop waves his halberd from the ramparts
and hollers:
        I want to turn my hand to the task and fell cedars,
        I want to earn eternal glory!

Then the Water-Sprite Michael talks about forestry management
in Lebanon. And then comes Škrhola with his dragon's head:
        Let me go free, Gilgamesh! Thou shalt be my lord
        and I thy servant. And the trees

I've grown for thee I now shall cut for thee
and I will build thee houses from them.

No sooner has Škrhola dropped dead decently
than the old dame cries out beneath the lime tree:
If thou wilt not create the Bull of Heaven
for me I'll smash the gates of the Nether World, shatter its hinges,
lead forth the dead
who will devour the living...
Then Doctor Faustus flings at her the Dragon's haunch
and Franz the Footman is exceedingly irate.

At this the puppeteer is greatly cheered
by all this action and, with ceaseless assurances
that this epic is a huge success,
chases all his puppets across the stage,
at random makes them wave their arms and legs
and in a mighty bass declaims the linking text,
so that Sumerian remnants float about in a verbal deluge;
and as he roars:
Who is the finest hero of them all,
who the most splendid of all men?
he kicks over the spotlight of the god Shamash
and through a total chaos ring the verses:
When he had travelled four times two hours
the darkness thickened, there's no light,
he can see nothing, either front or back,
when he had travelled five times two hours
the darkness thickened...

and nobody knows who is who,
torn is the curtain, and torn is the cap
of Punch, the children's friend,
and everyone goes home, no one knows where,
and in the box the Water-Sprite Michael, who on stage
escaped the worst,
quietly quotes Enkidu:
Heaven was calling,
Earth responded. And I stood all alone —
and then he adds: Blimey, this ain't half powerful,
this epic stuff. And anyway, we'll never
get such good parts again. Never.

# The autumnal bus

With an asthmatic puff the front door opens. Tripping on the steps the Passengers pour inside, collars turned up, weighed down with bags and bundles. Some are holding their glovers between their teeth. Others are squeezing their morning papers under their arms, feverishly searching for change. Passenger Nyklíčková is dragging a child by its hand but its feet keep slipping. Passenger Holas angrily shakes his fist at the darkness outside.

The Seated Passengers in Transit are watching with hostility.

Driver Chodura disgustedly turns his back on the steering wheel to check the Fares being dropped into the Coinbox, which displays a multitude of no longer valid fares.

Driver Chodura closes the door, which shuts with a creak. The lights go out.

The bus starts jerkily, the Passengers grope about and tumble into its depth. The bus is moving.

Driver Chodura turns to watch the last person drop in his Fare.

DRIVER CHODURA (*huskily*):
From stunted forests rises whitish steam...

SEATED PASSENGERS (*in chorus, with relief*):
for fishermen who have run out of stream,
for a black mirror with tenfold reflection...

PASSENGER HOLAS (*clasping a grab-hold*):
for empty veins of tracks and ancient highway sections...

STANDING PASSENGERS (*in chorus*):
for girls guarding dead geese in fields behind the byre,
for alien plumage in fastidious fire...

Honking, the Bus brakes, Passengers not holding on lurch forward. Driver Chodura spits through his half-open window.

DRIVER CHODURA (*with gusto*):
Snow ripens in the fists of unborn babes...

SEATED PASSENGERS (*some of them getting up to alight, in chorus*):
the spider in the eye-socket begins his tales...

PASSENGER NYKLÍČKOVÁ (*pushing her way through with her child, excitedly*):
The ice tree has sprung up and towards the sky will strain...

PASSENGER HOLAS (*at the door*):
we shall not meet upon this earth again.

SEATED PASSENGERS (*in chorus*):
We shall not meet upon this earth again.

DRIVER CHODURA (*braking, the lights come on*):
We shall not meet...

SEATED PASSENGERS (*in chorus*):
... upon this earth again.

The Bus has stopped, the door opens with a hiss and suddenly there is a deep and motionless silence.

PASSENGER NYKLÍČKOVÁ'S CHILD:
We shall not meet upon this earth again.

From a great distance comes the sound of honking, but otherwise the silence is unbroken. (Nobody moves.)

# The Angel of Death

In an indeterminate white space, which might equally be the gym of a rehabitational health institution as Purgatory, a double file of corpulent citizens $C_1 - C_n$ are riding exercise bicycles from right to left; in fact they remain stationary, pedalling. They wear white sweat-shirts and baggy suspicious-looking track-suit trousers. The citizens do not wriggle, do not look up, do not turn round and do not distract themselves; they just pedal on as if the regular running of the universe depended on it.

Above the row of bicycles hangs a good-sized loudspeaker which opens its black mouth and speaks in a sonorous, confidence-inspiring voice.

LOUDSPEAKER: Such then, citizens, is the mechanism of life. The union of sex cells is followed by explosive proliferation and differentiation. From the three germ layers develop tissues and organs, and already you have breathing, you have digestion, and little feet kicking...

The citizens pedal even more zealously.

LOUDSPEAKER: ...already fluids and factors are produced, already thinking begins, thoughts like glass fish in a black proto-sea.

One citizen cleans his ear with his little finger and they all keep pedalling.

LOUDSPEAKER: The self is distinguished from the non-self, a boundary now exists between the self and the world... The first cells mutate and degenerate, and the life clocks subtracts the first amount from the limited number of cell divisions. Birth now takes place. And leaving home... for schooling, training, culture. Exercise begins, and economic activity. Unflagging enthusiasm circulates from capillaries to the heart and back, if possible also through the lymphatic system. One walks cheerfully down sad streets and vice versa. One bets on the pools and new horizons open up. One makes love. The increased level of sex hormones ruins the thymus, control of malignant growth is reduced, malignancies occur, production of IgG antibodies is reduced, IgM antibodies cross-react with the body's own tissues, already we have rheumatism and collagen diseases, already atherosclerotic plaques appear in the coronary arteries, infarctions tap softly on the walls of the heart chambers...

The citizens, one after another, start pedalling at a furious rate, trying to ride away without moving from their spots.

LOUDSPEAKER: One walks sadly down sad streets, plaster falls. Even balconies fall. Maintenance has always been a problem.

Exhausted, the citizens revert to their original pace, wiping off their copious sweat in various ways.

LOUDSPEAKER: Freedom is recognised necessity. Here and there, cell division is exhausted. One is eating into one's capital. One jumps out of the way of buses. One plays the pools. Values are created. One works beyond retirement age. Culture is a function of work beyond retirement age. One turns inward. Inwardness is a function of muscular atrophies. Blood circulation is often insufficient. Especially in certain places. One embarks on a diet and on testosterone, and teeth are extracted. This is the time of wisdom and merits.

The citizens pedal on and suffer.

LOUDSPEAKER: And then, citizens, then... then comes the Angel of Death.

Darkness falls. A blood-red glow floods in from the sides. A heavy, fateful footfall is heard, rather like the monotonous sound of kettle-drums. The Angel of Death enters from the right. He is a slight little man in a rather shabby jacket and striped trousers made baggy by his knobbly knees. He has a drab briefcase and a bald head. He steps behind the last pair in such a way that none of the pedalling citizens can see him.

LOUDSPEAKER: Here's an opportunity for you, citizens. As a special treat from the management here's an opportunity for you. Speak to the Angel of Death, he's right behind you.

ANGEL OF DEATH (*suddenly yelling like a drill sergeant*): Comrades, atten-shun! And pedal on, citizens, pedal on. Let me tell you: exercise, exercise and again exercise. Only by exercise... Call that pedalling, Olejník?... you're sitting there like a baboon on a melon... Only by exercise do we consolidate our health... Come on, Opásek, pull those pants of yours up before they get entangled in your bloody chain... by consolidating our health and walking in the country in all weathers...Olejník, stop staring and keep pedalling...and also by willpower do we prevent illness. And preventing illness lengthens our lives. We want a long life...Opásek, have a new elastic put in or you'll never consolidate your health that way. We want a long life so that...well, Olejník? So that...

During the last few words the Angel of Death has fished out a cigarette from his breast pocket and lit it. He now blows the smoke at citizen Olejník who is in the last pair, directly in front of him.

Citizen Olejník dismounts from his exercise bicycle and turns to the Angel of Death.

OLEJNÍK (*timidly extends his hand*): Olejník, pleased to meet you, Mr...?

ANGEL OF DEATH: Karel Štác is my name.

They shake hands.
Citizen Olejník quietly crumples to the floor. The Angel of Death tucks his briefcase under his arm and gets on the vacant exercise bicycle.

ANGEL OF DEATH (*triumphantly*): So that we can longer still and better still...consolidate! So that we can longer still and better still...exercise! So we can prevent...! So we can longer still and better still...prolong! We keep pedalling and pedalling. So we can longer still and better still...

The Angel of Death chants the phrase rhythmically and the citizens adjust their pace, pedalling like a marching platoon, totally involved and with absolute confidence.

ANGEL OF DEATH (*pedalling and rhythmically chanting*): So we can longer still and better still...so we can longer still and better still...

# Crucifix

Behind the massive Bench, at the centre, sits the Judge in a threadbare gown. On both sides of him the Assessors, made of cardboard. Below the Bench, to the right, is the dock, were the Defendant is cringing: a small bird-like man, flanked by two beefy warders. Below the Bench, on the left, is the Prosecutor, standing erect and mostly addressing the public.

Above the Judge's head is a large crucifix, with a Crucified Christ of athletic build, his loincloth more like a pair of Bermuda shorts. Christ is smoking a huge cigar, puffing at it and from time to time tapping the ash in front of the Judge or on the Judge, holding the cigar in his nail-pierced and bleeding hand.

The proceedings are well-advanced.

PROSECUTOR: ... about these heinous crimes, yes, crimes, what is especially significant, yes, tremendously significant, is the defendant's pathological, though entirely conscious, and indeed calculated and calculating affection for animals. Yes, animals.

The Defendant cringes even more.

PROSECUTOR: In his flat he keeps—and this has been attested by witnesses and proved—he keeps three cats, twenty-eight mice, five of them white, one iguana and four, yes, four budgerigars. He looks after them and feeds them day and night. And this... this... person who has caused so much grief to his friends and neighbours and colleagues returns to his lair, in order to let white and grey mice out of their cages, in order to feed them on cheese, bacon, yes, and on bread and salt, and with his fingers, yes, fingers dirtied with so many machinations, to stroke the warty skin of an iguana...

The Defendant, visibly shaken, bows his head and covers his face.

PROSECUTOR: ... an iguana, in order to throw it dulled midges, yes midges, to treat it under an infra-red lamp, to fondle lazy and debauched cats and make them purr, yes, purr, while...

The Prosecutor suddenly stops as if he had forgotten his lines and lost his thread. He goes limp and looks anxious. At the same moment the Defendant abruptly stands erect. As if driven by the same mechanism the Prosecutor and the Defendant step out, in an almost ritualistic manner, and change places. The Court and the Warders do not move. The Defendant now stands in the Prosecutor's place and the Prosecutor sags and cringes between the two Warders.

DEFENDANT (*taking up naturally and without embarrassment*): ... while his colleagues and friends are collapsing under the weight of the evil done to them. Yet he cynically, yes, cynically...

The Defendant now towers high and, pointing his finger at the Prosecutor cringing between the Warders, raises his voice to a theatrical note:

DEFENDANT: ... feeds the crumbs which the mice have left to the budgerigars, giving the budgerigars sunflower seed, yes, seed, giving the budgerigars yesterday's rolls, and watches the sated love-birds preening themselves, yes, and billing and cooing. And that on a day when he had caused so much grief to his neighbours and colleagues... first of all by...

JUDGE (*snapping out of his tense concentration, shouting*): Keep to the point, please!

The Prosecutor glances up briefly but the Defendant is thundering on:

DEFENDANT: ... Yes, to the point. On the day when so many mice go hungry, when so many cats mew hopelessly on the roofs, when so many budgerigars are threatened, yes, directly threatened by atmospheric pollution and a shortage of sunflowers, on the day when some iguanas, yes, iguanas, are literally becoming extinct, yes, physically extinct, on the day when, for instance, only two specimens of the iguana *Ophisalis corneliana* survive and, moreover, neither knows about the other!

The Defendant falls silent and looks around triumphantly. The Judge looks slowly at his watch.

JUDGE (*shouting hysterically*): Silence in Court! The case is adjourned. The Court will retire for consultation. Remain in your seats. The hearing will resume at ten o'clock.

The Judge rises. He is not very tall; his gown sits on him strangely. The Warders rise too, march up behind the Bench and grab the Judge by his shoulders. Carelessly they drag him out of the courtroom. The Judge wriggles feebly in their grip.

The Prosecutor and Defendant walk up to each other, offer each other a cigarette, light up, and quietly whisper together.

Christ chucks away his cigar and spits conspicuously.

PROSECUTOR: ... No, 'is nerves ain't what they used to be. Why, under Disraeli—did ya know that?—we 'ad even trained crickets and eight squirrels.

DEFENDANT: That ain't nothing. Why, under Vespasian I even threw in a couple of young tigers.

CHRIST (*nervously*): I say, boys, give me a hand down, will you?

The Prosecutor pulls himself out of his reverie, turns and with deliberate superiority snaps:

PROSECUTOR: You're the last straw! Just hang on up there!

# Supper à la Russell Edson

The most ordinary kitchen imaginable. A gas cooker, shelves. In the middle a table laid for a meal, its short side against the wall. At the other short side, facing the wall, sits the Child. The Mother moves from the cooker to the table with a bowl from which rises a steady cloud of steam, as from an oracle's cauldron. On the chair facing the door is a cushion and sitting on it a huge egg-shaped stone—granite, gneiss or a coping stone. Just as Mother has placed the dish on the table the door opens abruptly and Father rolls in, wearing an overcoat and scarf, and a modish hat pulled well down. At his entry the lights go up considerably and it becomes obvious that Father, Mother and the Child are wearing masks with a mildly comical grin.

FATHER: What's this then?

MOTHER: What's what? Good evening.

FATHER: What's that stone there?

MOTHER: A stone.

FATHER: Okay. What's it doing on my chair?

MOTHER: We invited it for supper.

FATHER: Who's we?

MOTHER: ... Well... we.

FATHER: Don't talk rot. Put it away. It's on my chair.

MOTHER: We invited it for supper. There's no other chair, and you weren't here.

CHILD: He's going to play with me after supper.

FATHER: Shut up! That's my place and no one's going to loll about in it. That's my place, even if I wasn't here at all. It's my place even if I spat at it only once a year. Put him away. That's my place even if I dangled from the ceiling.

MOTHER: Don't shout. We have a guest. You'll spoil his appetite.

FATHER: I didn't invite him. I didn't... Where am I to sit? What d'you suggest I do?

MOTHER: If you went past the window outside you'd be a pleasant passer-by. If you lay down by the stove you'd make a pretty pattern on the lino. If you crawled into that pot you could be a potato.

CHILD: You could sprout. I'd water you.

FATHER: Shut up! Okay. So you like that chunk of rock better than me?

MOTHER: He's... We don't like him specially at all. We just invited him for supper.

FATHER: What have you got going with him? You don't just invite...

MOTHER: There's nothing between us. He's... He just was so on his own...

FATHER: I'm on my own too.

CHILD: Go out, then... Maybe somebody'll find you.

FATHER: Shut up!

CHILD: And he's...

MOTHER: Behave yourself. You'll spoil his appetite. You'll upset his digestion. I can't stand stones with indigestion.

FATHER: I don't give a damn about what you can't stand. This is my place and this is my food.

CHILD: But he's...

MOTHER: When we've eaten you can take a bit out into the hall with you. Or to the stove. Or to the ceiling.

CHILD: But he's got a golden vein, did you know?

FATHER: ... So... Okay. So you've found a replacement for me.

MOTHER: We weren't looking for anything. You weren't looking for anything either.

CHILD: I wasn't looking for anything either.

FATHER: Shut up! Are you saying that over all these years I forgot to replace myself?

120

MOTHER: I'm not saying anything. I haven't been saying anything for ages. I don't know anything.

FATHER: Okay. I didn't replace myself, so you now have a replacement. I'm to lie down in the corner and wait. Okay. You're not saying anything. Okay. You don't know anything. You don't even know whose place this is or who I am.

MOTHER: I'm just dishing up the supper.

Mother lifts the lid off the dish, and even greater clouds of steam pour out, engulfing the room. With a curse Father whips off his scarf and hat, steps up to the table facing the stone and takes off his mask. He has no face: his head is made of exactly the same stone as that sitting opposite him.

Mother freezes in her movement over the dish. The Child leaps to his feet. As if on command they both take off their masks. They too, understandably, have shapeless stones instead of faces.

MOTHER: (*with relief, pushing Father out of the way*): I'm just dishing up the supper.

# Sand game

A corner of a park. Fragrant shrubs of jasmine (or mock-orange blossom). In the centre a sandpit, somewhat churned up, beyond it a spattered seat of unpainted wood. Hidden among the shrubs, but visible, is a wooden shed, into which one can see through its wrenched-off door. It contains shovels, hoes, wheelbarrows and spilled sacks of something or other.

On the seat sits a relatively young Oldster with white hair, in a leather jacket and turtleneck shirt. He is reading a newspaper which he holds permanently open in front of him, without lowering it. From time to time he peers over the top of it.

Playing in the sandpit are two relatively big children: Ilona and Robert. They have built a rather elaborate structure of sand, bits of board, wire and dogshit. It suggests a rocket launching site or the hanging gardens of Babylon.

OLDSTER (*peering over his paper*): It says here it'll be windy with heavy showers. That'll sweep that nonsense of yours away all right!

ROBERT: That isn't actually possible. The anticyclone is still over Norway. We are still under the influence of a fairly substantial high, which is only slowly shifting to the south.

OLDSTER (*irritably*): But that's what it says here!

ILONA: The structure is sufficiently solidly anchored. We considered all the parameters. This linkage here will stand up to a pressure of 50 grammes per square centimetre. The tolerances are considerable.

OLDSTER (*even more irritably*): You can't make something from nothing. I don't care what tol... tol... tolerances you've got. There'll be a downpour. It says so here.

ROBERT (*adding another piece of wood*): The information flow is often overlaid by a considerable amount of noise. It is necessary to relate the general and summary estimate to the specific system which represents only a small segment of the reality covered by the information frame. More particularly: the microclimatic conditions of this sandpit can be defined only on the basis of physical evidence regarding the maximum number of parameters of the ambient formation.

ILONA (*adding a sand patty*): Besides, even the essence of the artifact itself changes reality, or let us say micro-reality, to the extent that information pre-dating its creation cannot be fully valid, that is: true, after its creation.

ROBERT: This is an analogous situation to any anagenetic effect under natural conditions, which are never identical in relation to the new object, nor in relation to themselves once the object has passed from the sphere of intellectual conception to the sphere of physical realisation.

OLDSTER: You're mad. There was a blood-red sunset yesterday and the birds are flying low. It says here a bridge collapsed in Ecuador. No, wait a minute... not in Ecuador, but in what's-its-name... in Puerto Rico, no, in Malay... Malay... no, in Belgium.

ILONA (*to Robert*): A few deep injections are needed at this point.

ROBERT (*to Ilona*): Quite right. The added height might otherwise result in such stress that, with the given material, we might exceed the original parameters.

OLDSTER (*angrily*): You're mad. He that mischief hatches mischief catches, don't you worry, no matter how much you... you parametrify yourself!

ROBERT (*straightening up, but with the patience typical of his age*): In substantial thinking we certainly can relate the value of essence, or even the value of its actual statement, to a certain preformed model, with regard to which that essence of statement then appears, in some way or other, insufficient, inadequate, or indeed excessive. In such a case we may then employ verbal comparisons through which we release dissatisfaction, or frustration, caused by the immanence of the preconceived model in our thinking, no matter how we perceive it...

OLDSTER: Mad as a hatter!

ILONA: But he is, moreover, and in my opinion rightly, a believer in non-substantial ontology...

ROBERT (*starts walking up and down and expounding in the manner of the Platonic school*): ... because it alone enables us to free ourselves from the rigid structures of the old or new anthropological reductionism and to reconstruct our world both in terms of its phenomenology and of its freely and operationally substituted existentiality...

OLDSTER (*waving his paper*): Oh, go to... It says here...

ROBERT (*in mounting ecstasy which causes the appearance of slight flickering and sparking around his head, eventually encircling his head as a kind of permanent greenish glow*): ... reconstruct our world in its meaningful comprehensiveness, and that with full realisation of our involvement, and hence from within the field we are trying to comprehend, but also, up to a point, on the basis of abstraction from our own participation, on the basis of self-objectivisation and ad hoc derealisation, which of course is the beginning of genuine and permanent realisation...

OLDSTER: You're quite mad!

ROBERT (*in his ecstasy he enters the shed, complete with halo, stumbling over the junk until he is lost from sight*): ... so that the reconstruction of the world in the system of non-substantial ontology...

From the shed comes the sound of an explosion, some pieces of timber fly out and clouds of black dirt. Ilona sits down on the sand construction and flattens it. The Oldster jumps up, shielding his head with his paper. As the noise and smoke subside a somewhat shaken Robert, now minus his halo, crawls out of the shed.

OLDSTER (*triumphantly*): Didn't I say you were mad?

124

**Miroslav Holub** was born in 1923. He is not only Czechoslovakia's most important poet, but also one of her leading scientists, working as a research immunologist in Prague. He did not write poetry at all until he started clinical research at the age of thirty.

Holub was first introduced to English readers with a *Selected Poems* (1967) in the Penguin Modern European Poets series, in translations by Ian Milner and George Theiner. Ian and Jarmila Milner translated two further collections published here, *Although* (Cape, 1971) and *Notes of a Clay Pigeon* (Secker, 1977). The Secker volume was a selection of poems from *Naopak*, a collection published in Czechoslovakia in 1982. *On the Contrary and Other Poems* presents a decade of Holub's work, combining the *Naopak* poems with work from a new book, *Interferon čili o divadle* [Interferon or On the Theatre], parts of which are currently being read or performed on stage at the Viola Poetry Theatre in Prague.

**Ewald Osers** was born in 1917 in Prague, and has lived in Britain since 1938. After studying chemistry and then Slavonic languages, he worked for the BBC Monitoring Service from 1939 to 1977. He has translated poetry and prose from Czech, Slovak, German, Bulgarian, Russian and Serbo-Croat; in 1971 he received the Schlegel-Tieck Prize for German translation, and in 1977 the International C.B. Nathorst Translation Prize.

His anthologies include *Three Czech Poets* [Nezval, Bartušek, Hanzlík] in the Penguin Modern European Poets series (1970). He has translated two collections by Jaroslav Seifert, *The Plague Column* (Terra Nova Editions, 1979) and *Umbrella from Piccadilly* (London Magazine Editions, 1983), as well as Antonin Bartušek's *The Aztec Calendar and Other Poems* (Anvil Press, 1975), and books by Ondra Lysohorsky, Reiner Kunze, Hans Dieter Schäfer, Rose Ausländer, Rudolf Langer and Walter Helmut Fritz.